MADE IN THE
U.S.A.

Golf Balls
From Start to Finish

Ryan A. Smith

Photographs by Gary Tolle

BLACKBIRCH PRESS
An imprint of Thomson Gale, a part of The Thomson Corporation

THOMSON
GALE

Detroit • New York • San Francisco • San Diego • New Haven, Conn. • Waterville, Maine • London • Munich

LIBRARY OF CONGRESS CATALOGING-IN-PUBLICATION DATA

Smith, Ryan A., 1974–
   Golf balls / by Ryan A. Smith.
      p. cm. — (Made in the USA)
   Includes bibliographical references and index.
   ISBN 1-4103-0657-7 (hard cover : alk. paper)
   1. Golf balls. I. Title. II. Series: Made in the U.S.A.

GV976.G64 2005
796.352'028—dc22   2005006320

Contents

Special Thanks
Special thanks to John Steinbach, Eric Loper, Gary Tolle, Charles Martin, Jim Guerrero, Herbert Heffernan, Sanjay Kuttappa, and the hundreds of people working at the TaylorMade-adidas Golf Company.

Golf Balls

The game of golf was invented in Scotland during the late 1400s. At first, the tiny balls used to play golf were made by hand of solid wood. Over the centuries, people have used golf balls made of goose feathers stitched inside pieces of leather, sap from tropical trees, packing materials, solid rubber, and even wound-up rubber bands! Most golf balls today, though, are constructed of space-age materials and made inside huge production factories.

But how exactly are golf balls made?

Most golf balls today are made of space-age plastics inside large factories.

3

Maxfli

Maxfli, part of the TaylorMade-adidas Golf Company, is one of the leading manufacturers of golf balls in the world. Maxfli has sold millions of golf balls during its long history with the sport.

Many different kinds of golf balls are made by Maxfli. Some are designed to fly far, others to fly high. Some balls are designed for beginner and amateur players to use, while others are designed for specific pro golfers to use. But no matter what new golf ball Maxfli produces, every one is first created at its facility in Carlsbad, California.

Maxfli makes many different types of golf balls (opposite). Professional golfers like Sergio Garcia (left) have golf balls specially designed for them.

Research and Development

The first step in making any golf ball begins in the research and development (R&D) department. The R&D engineers design every golf ball made by Maxfli. Initially, engineers use science and math to experiment with the different materials used to make golf balls. Computers and machines are used together to collect data about the flexibility, durability, and hardness of the different plastics and rubbers.

R&D engineers experiment with the rubber and plastic compounds used to make the different layers (left) of golf balls. The Iron Byron machine (opposite) creates a perfect swing to test balls at Maxfli.

One machine engineers use to test finished golf balls is called Iron Byron. Iron Byron is a giant mechanical arm that hits a ball perfectly with a golf club. As Iron Byron hits a golf ball, high-speed cameras and computers gather information about the ball's predicted flight pattern.

Iron Byron was designed to replicate the golf swing of pro golfer Byron Nelson. But Iron Byron can hit a golf ball faster than 180 miles per hour!

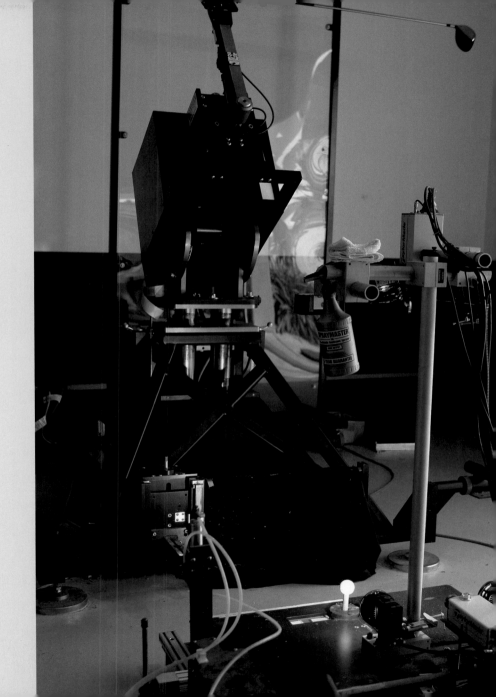

Raw rubber arrives in enormous 70-pound bricks called bales.

Creating Cores with Rubber

The base material used to make the center, or core, of any solid golf ball is rubber. Solid golf balls are the most popular in play today. Solid balls are formed from two to four molded layers of rubber and plastic.

Raw rubber arrives at Maxfli in large, 70-pound (31.75-kilogram) bricks called bales. To begin making cores, chunks cut from a rubber bale are mixed with a blend of powdered fillers using a heated mill. The new mixture exits the mill as a colorful, flat sheet that resembles dough. Engineers use the different-colored mixtures to tell them which kind of core they are working with.

A heated mill mixes raw rubber with powdered fillers (above) until the mixture is completely blended (inset).

The Extruder

The flattened mixture must be rolled into a tube shape before it is loaded into the extruder machine. The rolled mixture is compacted inside the extruder and slowly forced out a small, round hole.

As the extruder rams the mixture out, sharp blades automatically slice it into cylinder-shaped chunks called preps.

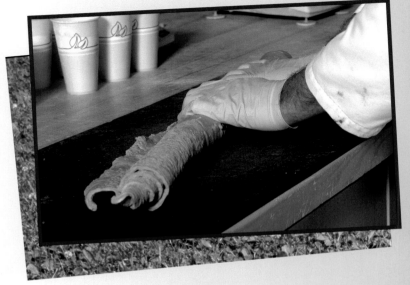

Opposite: *The core mixture looks like flattened dough before it is loaded into the extruder machine.*

Above Left: *The mixture is rolled into a tubelike shape.*

Above Right: *The rolled mixture is placed into the extruder.*

Right: *The extruder cuts cylinder-shaped preps as the mixture is pushed out.*

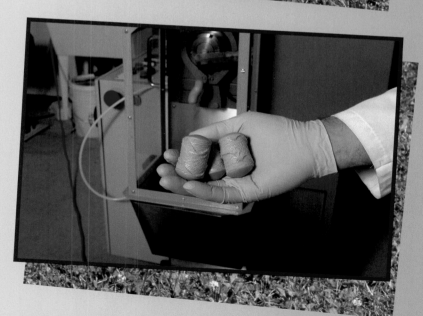

Above Left: *Preps are loaded into the compression machine.*

Above Right: *Intense heat and pressure are applied inside the machine.*

Left: *The new cores stick to the roof of the machine when it is opened.*

Opposite: *The excess material surrounding each core must be removed.*

The Compression Machine

The preps are placed in steel molds inside a compression machine. Intense heat and pressure are applied to the preps inside the machine to mold them into the round cores of golf balls. The high temperature also creates a chemical reaction within the core mixture that hardens the cores as they cool.

The cores are extracted from the molds as they cool. Any excess material left on the cores is ground off so they all form perfect spheres.

Making Mantles

The middle layer, or mantle, of a three-piece solid golf ball is made of special plastics and fillers. The plastics arrive in the form of tiny pellets and the fillers are powders.

First, the pellets are combined with fillers inside a heated barrel machine. The mixture is crushed and heated into a lavalike consistency inside the barrel.

Plastic pellets are mixed with powdered fillers in a heated barrel machine.

The Mold Base

While the pellets and fillers are being heated, the cores are placed in steel cavities inside a mold base. Tiny pins extending from the tops and bottoms of the cavities hold the cores perfectly centered.

Top: Cores are set inside steel cavities in a mold base.

Bottom: Each cavity contains two sets of pins to hold the cores in place.

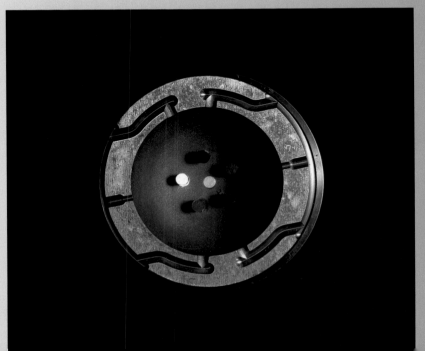

15

Molding Mantles

The lavalike plastic mixture from the heated barrel is then injected into the cores through a series of channels in the mold base. One-eighth-inch (3.17-millimeter) gaps between the cores and cavity walls exist inside the closed mold base. In less than one second, the mantle mixture flows into the cavity spaces, the pins automatically retract, and the cores become suspended inside the molten mantle.

Mantles are formed with an advanced molding machine (left). Inside the machine, the lavalike mixture injected into the mold base (opposite) surrounds the cores.

The Degater

The new mantles harden and become solid as they cool. When the mold base is opened, the cooled mantles inside are connected by hardened plastic, called gates, left inside the channels. A device called a degater uses knifelike blades to cut the gates from the mantles. The separated mantles are washed before they move on.

Opposite: *A degater is used to separate the plastic gates from the mantles.*

Above and Right: *Newly molded mantles are inserted into a degater to completely remove the gates.*

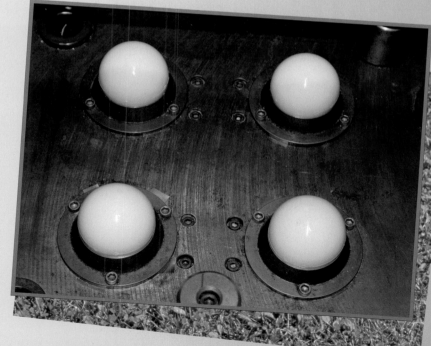

Molding Covers

A clean mantle receives a third layer, or cover, in the same way the core received the mantle. The cover is the hard plastic shell of a golf ball.

One difference in the cover-molding process, though, is that the cavities inside this mold base have raised dimple patterns. Balls with dimple patterns on their surface fly farther and straighter than balls with smooth surfaces. Another difference in the cover-molding process is the materials used. Cover-molding requires very hard, scuff-resistant plastics. Tiny chunks of color are also mixed in with the plastic to ultimately give the covers a flat white look.

Mantles are placed into a different mold base (below) to create the cover layer. These cavities create dimpled patterns (opposite and inset) on the surface of the new golf balls.

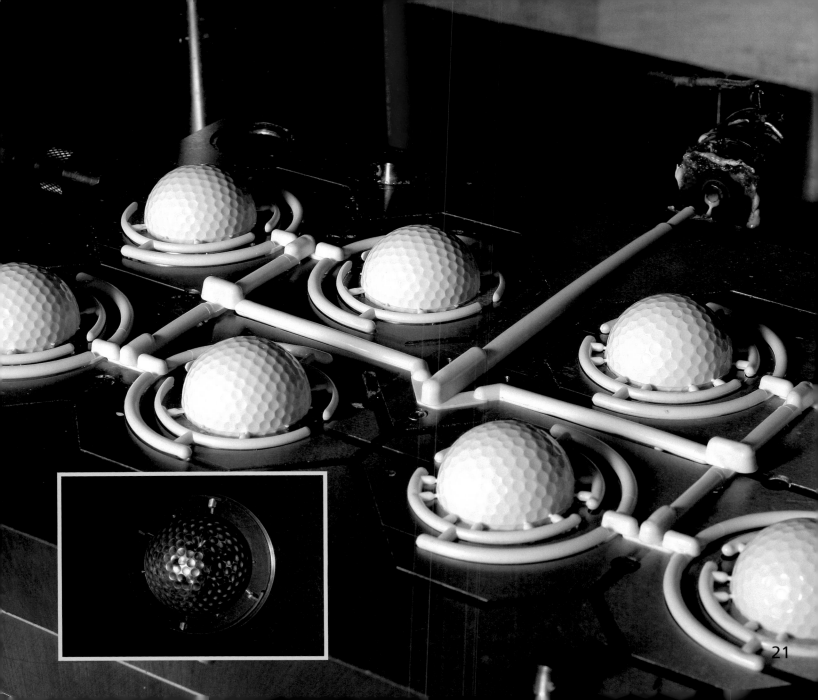

The Evolution of Golf Balls

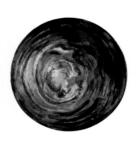

Over the centuries, the balls used in golf have continuously improved, and they are still evolving today. The first modern golf balls were wooden. Balls fashioned from Scotland's hardwood trees, such as beech or box-root, were popular for almost 200 years. However, they did not work very well and softened in wet conditions.

In 1618, golf balls handcrafted of stitched leather and feathers were introduced. Three wet pieces of leather were sewn together to form a hollow ball with a small opening. Boiled goose feathers were jammed into the leather shell and then it was sewn shut. As it dried, the leather shrank, and the feathers expanded as they dried. The result was a surprisingly hard and round golf ball.

The next generation of golf balls, Gutty balls, were introduced in 1848. They were made from the sap of tropical trees like the gutta. The sap was heated, rolled into balls, and smoothed on a wooden board. The cooled sap became quite hard, perfect for a golf ball.

Around this time, people discovered that dinged golf balls often flew straighter and farther than smooth balls. After 1880, most Gutties were produced with bumps or patterns hammered or pressed onto their surface. These balls led to the dimple patterns on golf balls used today!

Around 1900, the first golf balls made with rubber were invented. Inside each ball, hundreds of feet of rubber thread were wound around a solid rubber core. The wound rubber-band balls were covered with hard shells made of gutta tree sap.

Many improvements over the past hundred years have continued the evolution of golf balls. From space-age rubbers and plastics to computerized molding processes to beyond, golf ball technology is sure to move forward in the future.

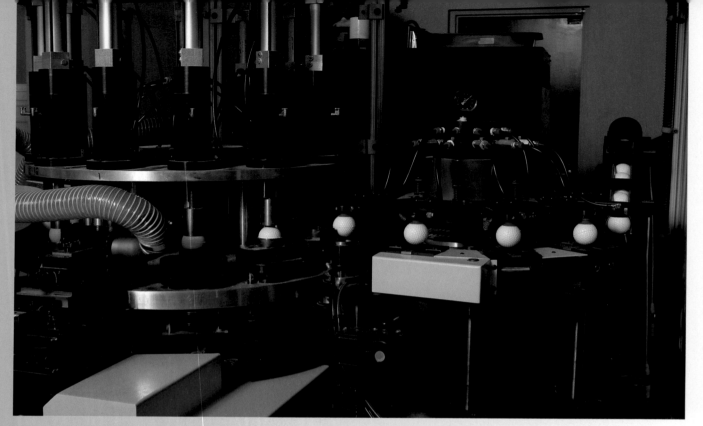

The seam-buffing machine (above) removes the seam and any plastic bumps (opposite) left on the golf balls during the cover-molding process.

The Seam-Buffing Machine

Covered golf balls all go through the seam-buffing machine. Inside it, the balls are rotated as they move through a variety of sanding and polishing stations. Sanding and polishing removes any raised plastic bumps and seams left on the covers during the molding process.

Prepare for Paint

Before they can be covered in paint, buffed golf balls must be thoroughly cleaned. A large washing machine uses vibration and pressure blasts of water to remove any particles of dust, residue, and dirt from the balls. Cleaning the balls thoroughly ensures that the paint can be applied evenly and flawlessly.

A large washing machine uses water and vibration to thoroughly clean each golf ball.

A stamping machine prints the Maxfli logo onto a golf ball.

Printing Logos

An ink logo of the Maxfli brand name is stamped onto each golf ball just before paint is applied. Stamping machines print logos onto the balls using an automatic pad-and-ink process. After the ink dries, the balls are carefully transported to the paint room.

Left: *Each golf ball is set onto a spindle in the paint room.*

Opposite Top and Bottom: *A long line of spindles quickly carries the balls past a series of paint guns.*

A single painting machine can paint more than 57,000 balls in an eight-hour workday.

28

Paint Room

In the paint room, golf balls are placed, one at a time, onto a very long row of tiny spindles. The spindles rotate 360 degrees and are attached to a moving track. The track leads the row of turning balls through a small room of angled paint guns. As the balls spin, streams of clear paint completely cover them. The coatings of clear paint will give the balls a glossy white look. The clear paint also prevents the balls from being stained by grass and protects the logo from scuffing.

Quality Control

Every Maxfli golf ball must pass a quality inspection before it can be sold. Workers use special machines to inspect each ball for material flaws. One machine ensures all the balls are the correct size and weight. Regulation golf balls must not be wider than 1.68 inches (4.2cm) or weigh more than 1.62 ounces (45.9g).

Every golf ball must pass a quality inspection before it can be packaged.

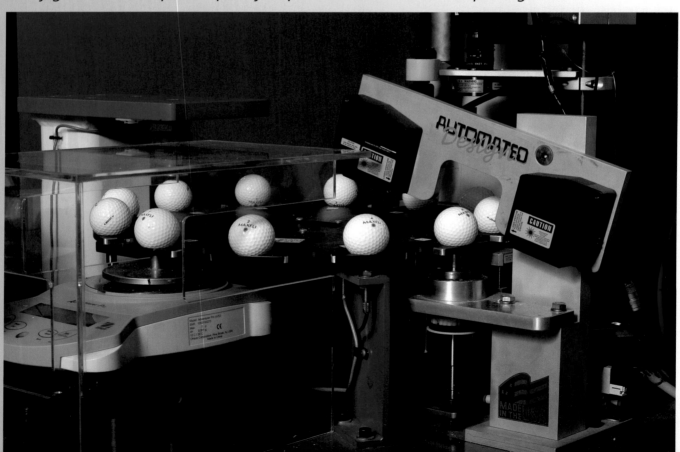

End of the Line

Golf balls that pass inspection are packaged and prepared for shipment. Three Maxfli balls at a time are placed into small, narrow boxes called sleeves. Four sleeves are loaded into a larger box, and the balls are sent to retail stores by the dozen.

From there, Maxfli balls are sold to an estimated 60 million golfers worldwide to replace the 2.5 billion golf balls they lose on courses every year.

Once approved, golf balls are packaged into sleeves and boxes of twelve to be sold in pro shops around the world.

Glossary

Channels Tube-shaped passages in the mold base

Core The center of a solid golf ball

Cover The hard, dimpled plastic shell of a golf ball

Degater A machine that removes the plastic gates left behind during molding

Dimples Tiny indents molded onto the surface of golf ball covers

Extruder A machine that makes preps from the rolled rubber mixture

Iron Byron A mechanical arm used to test golf balls

Mantle The middle layer of a three-piece golf ball

Preps Compressed, cylindrical chunks of rubber that exit the extruder

Sleeve A small, narrow box that holds three new golf balls

For More Information

Books

Jim Corbett, *The Golf Book for Kids.* Seattle, WA: Hara, 2000.

Betty Moore, *The Baffled Parents Guide to Teaching Kids Golf.* Camden, ME: Ragged Mountain Press, 2001.

Web Sites

TaylorMade-adidas Golf Company (www.taylormadeadidasgolf.com). Find out more about the golf equipment made by the TaylorMade-adidas Golf Company at their official Web site.

U.S. Kids Golf (www.uskidsgolf.com). Get fitted with the perfect golf equipment for kids of all ages and sizes, as well as find family golf courses and tournaments across the country or in your neighborhood.

GolfOnline (http://sportsillustrated.cnn.com/golfonline/beginners/direct/forkids.html). Designed just for kids, this Web site features golf instruction for beginners, a history of the game, rules, etiquette tips, and golf terms.

Index